STO

FRIENDS
OF ACPL

**DO NOT REMOVE
CARDS FROM POCKET**

CHESSIE
THE
LONG ISLAND SQUIRREL
A True Story

For a free color catalog describing Gareth Stevens' list of high-quality children's books, call 1-800-341-3569 (USA) or 1-800-461-9120 (Canada).

Library of Congress Cataloging-in-Publication Data

Komoto, Sachiko, 1940-
    [Okasan ni natti risu no Chibi. English]
    Chessie the Long Island squirrel / by Sachiko Komoto. --
North American ed.
       p. cm.
    Translation of: Okasan ni natti risu no Chibi.
    Summary: Follows Chessie the squirrel through the four
seasons, from infancy to motherhood.
    ISBN 0-8368-0198-9
    1. Squirrels--Juvenile fiction. [1. Squirrels--Fiction.]
I. Title.
PZ10.3.K784Ch 1992
[E]--dc20   90-46860

North American edition first published in 1992 by
Gareth Stevens Publishing
1555 North RiverCenter Drive, Suite 201
Milwaukee, Wisconsin 53212, USA

English text: MaryLee Knowlton

Printed in MEXICO

1 2 3 4 5 6 7 8 9 97 96 95 94 93 92

CHESSIE
THE
LONG ISLAND SQUIRREL
A True Story

Sachiko Komoto

Gareth Stevens Publishing
MILWAUKEE

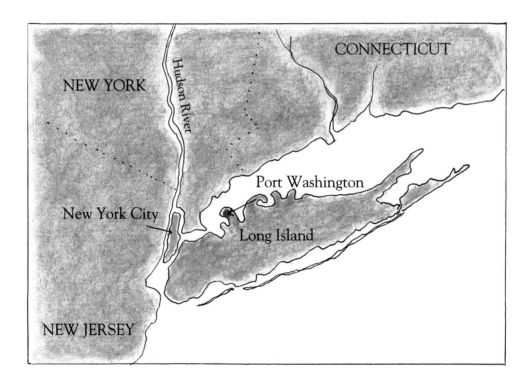

Harry lived in the small town of Port Washington, just outside of New York City. His house was surrounded by great leafy oak trees, and maples and beeches grown old and grand.

One winter, a family of gray squirrels moved into Harry's yard. Throughout the changing seasons of the year, he watched the squirrels grow. The littlest squirrel, with patches of red fur on her cheeks, was Harry's favorite, and he called her Chessie. This is the story of Chessie's first year.

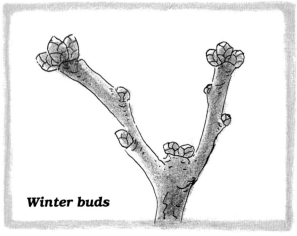

Winter buds

The winter had been harsh. In February, the trees still stood black and bare against the sunless, gray sky. The world was frozen and almost silent.

But in the old oak tree, something was stirring. Since late December, a squirrel had been nesting in a hole high on the trunk. Sometimes she left her nest to hop from branch to branch among the trees in the yard.

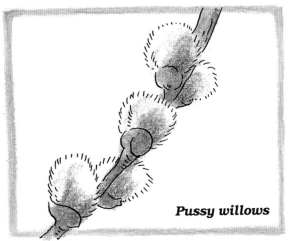

Pussy willows

In mid-March, five baby squirrels were born in the hole in the old oak. The mother squirrel didn't run through the trees any more. Day after day, she stayed in the nest, nursing her babies and washing them with her tongue.

One day, the hungry mother squirrel left her nest to search for food. She hadn't eaten since her babies were born. She tasted the winter buds on her oak tree, but they were still too hard to eat.

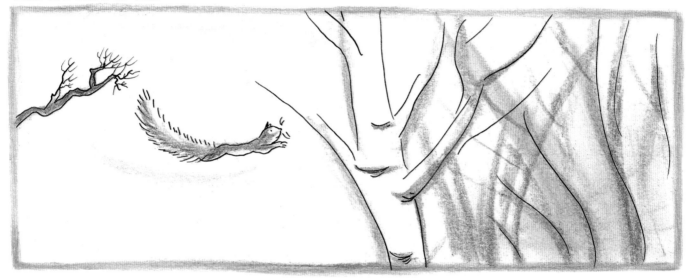

Anxiously, she scampered from tree to tree eating any soft buds she could find. Her babies were waiting for her.

High, squeaky cries greeted the mother squirrel when she returned. She wrapped her babies in her fluffy, warm tail and nursed and licked them until they all fell asleep.

One day in April, the baby squirrels poked their heads out of the nest for the first time. From his window, Harry watched as the littlest one, with red fur on her cheeks, nearly tumbled from the tree. This was Chessie.

Suddenly, a large, black bird appeared in a whir of great wings. The mother squirrel returned in a flash, chattering and scolding the bird, ready to fight off any danger to her babies.

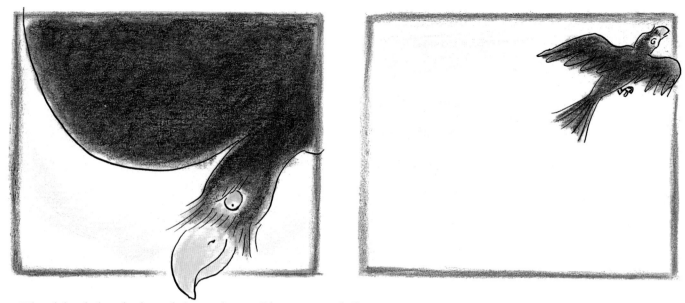

The black bird glared fiercely at Chessie and flew away.

But the mother squirrel knew he would be back to try and catch her babies.
They would have to move someplace safer.

She searched the yard for a place to build a new nest.

In a corner of the yard, she found an early-blooming maple with a good hole in it. The clusters of spring buds would hide the hole from the black bird's sight. The mother squirrel swiftly cleaned old twigs and leaves from the hole. Then she dashed down the trunk to find something to line the nest.

The mother squirrel's strong teeth pulled dry grass from the foot of an oak tree. As she glanced up, she spied something else she could use!

Hanging from the oak tree's branch, Harry's old tire swing dangled at the end of a strong hemp rope. The mother squirrel jumped onto the tire and began to shred the rope with her sharp teeth.

Then she jumped to the ground, her cheek pouches stuffed with rope fibers. Back to the maple tree she streaked,

and up the trunk. She spread the fibers on the floor to make her new nest soft.

She returned again and again to the rope to fill her pouches until — *clump!* — the tire fell to the ground. The new nest would be a cozy cradle for her babies.

Moving day had come. As the early sun lit the yard, the mother squirrel's face appeared at the opening of the old nest. Her nose twitched as she sniffed the air for worrisome scents. Her ears pricked up and her eyes darted around the yard, on the alert for danger. Satisfied that no danger was near, she picked up Chessie by the scruff of her neck and headed down the tree trunk.

When the mother squirrel reached the ground, she looked cautiously all around her. She ran a few steps, then stopped and checked again. Running and checking, running and checking, she finally reached the maple tree. She dropped Chessie into the soft, new nest and ran back to the old oak for the next baby. After four more trips, the gray squirrel family was tucked safely into its new home.

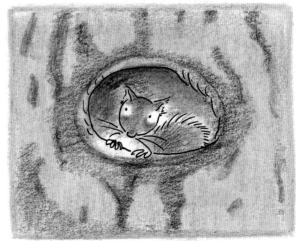

The new nest, with its pillow of soft hemp, was very comfortable. And there was no sign of the black bird. But now the mother squirrel had a new worry. Her babies wanted to explore. Chattering noisily, she pushed four of them back into the nest. But where was Chessie?

Ah, there she was — about three feet from the nest. She was frozen with fear, unable to turn around and come back. The mother squirrel snatched Chessie up and popped her back into the nest.

But in a twinkling, Chessie was out again. This time, her mother didn't bring her back. Instead, she taught Chessie how to turn around.

As the days passed, the little squirrels moved around more and more. Soon they needed more food than just their mother's milk. It was time to move again — this time to a tree with tender new leaves for the babies to eat.

All the trees were covered with buds. Where would the mother squirrel find one whose leaves were already out?

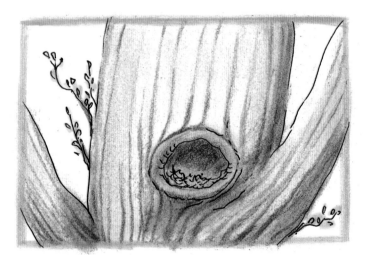 

Ah! An elm tree with soft, new leaves! And a hole. Out with the old leaves! In with the soft, dried grass!

Five trips with five baby squirrels!

The squirrel family was home again. By day, the little squirrels feasted on tender elm leaves. And at night, they curled up with their mother and nursed.

19

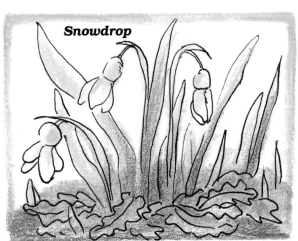

Snowdrop

Spring was in bloom. Snowdrops peeked out, tiny and white. Soon, the first crocus pushed through the sun-warmed soil.

The yard bustled with springtime activities. Bees, robins — even a turtle — had business to tend to. Harry and his family began to clean up the yard after the long winter.

Crocus

The May winds blew in, damp and warm,

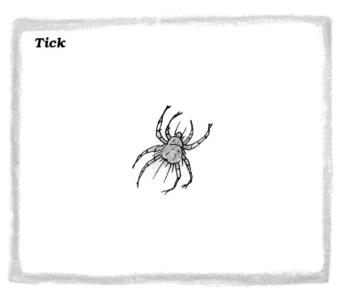

Tick

and the little squirrels were growing too big for their nest. Fleas and ticks began to bite the squirrels as the nest grew cramped and dirty.

So it was time to move to a summer nest in a beech tree. In summer, its lovely leaves would shelter the nest. And in fall, its branches would grow heavy with nuts for the squirrels' winter food.

 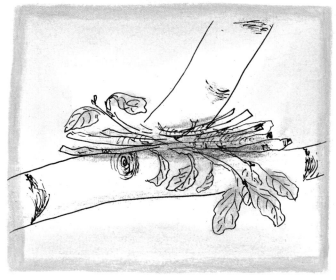

The mother squirrel picked a beech tree at the edge of the yard. Then she began to build the summer nest — first a few sticks on a fat branch,

 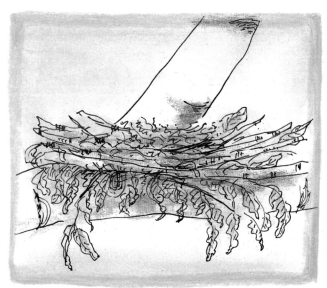

then some dried grass and moss on top, and the summer home was ready.

The last night in the maple tree, the little squirrels slept soundly, wrapped in their mother's big tail. The next day, they would move to their new nest on the beech tree branch. Only this time, their mother would not carry them.

Daybreak. As the sun shone through the morning mist, the mother squirrel roused her babies.

She twitched her nose. No strange scents. Five little squirrels twitched five little noses. They didn't smell anything, either.

The mother squirrel listened and looked. Five pairs of ears pricked up and five pairs of eyes darted around. All clear.

Signaling with a low chirp, the mother squirrel headed down the maple tree trunk. Five little squirrels followed. Little Chessie came last of all, running fast to keep up with the others.

The mother squirrel reached the ground and dashed behind a stump, five babies close behind her. The next part would be tricky. They must cross the open lawn.

At the mother squirrel's low chirp, the squirrel family streaked across the grass, still slippery with morning dew.

Up the trunk they clambered and tumbled into their new nest. The little squirrels had made this move on their very own legs!

The new nest swayed in the wind like a cradle. Chessie learned to eat the young leaves and the delicious insect eggs that clung to the branches.

Beech tree branch

Throughout the late spring, the mother squirrel taught her babies to clean their fur to remove loose hairs and fleas and ticks. The squirrels were particularly fussy about their tails. They combed them using their front paws and teeth. They scratched them with their back paws. All this care kept five little tails clean and bushy.

The mother squirrel also taught the little squirrels how to balance using their tails like parachutes as they jumped from tree to tree.

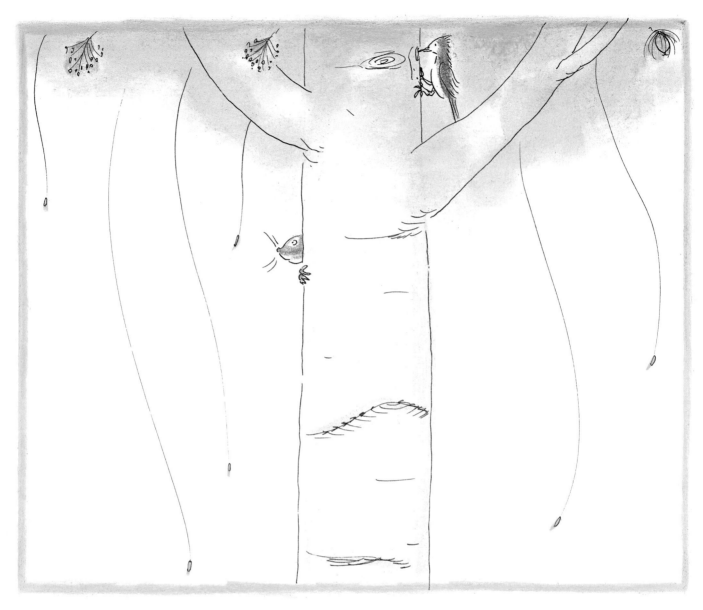

One day, Chessie saw a green thing hanging by a thread from the beech tree.
She stretched out her paw to grab it, but the breeze swung the green thing out
of her reach.

That night, a hard wind blew.

When morning came, little green things were scattered all over the ground, blown down by the night wind. They were insect larvae, grown from the eggs stuck on the tree branches. The mother squirrel and her babies joined the birds in a delicious, nutritious feast.

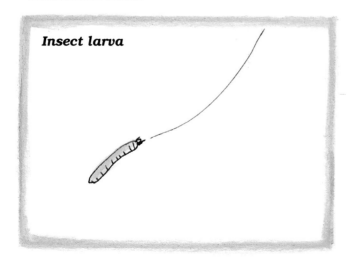

Insect larva

Chessie was becoming
quite bold and very curious.

She sniffed a flower, but not the bee.

A baseball *looked* tasty.   But it wasn't.

Cat food would do in a pinch.

But the cat didn't want to share.

Chessie dashed up a tree and out on a branch, followed by the angry cat.
Her tail flying behind her, Chessie jumped to a windowsill out of the cat's reach.

She found herself at Harry's window.

"Have a walnut," said Harry. Chessie gobbled it down.

Then she was off, flying through the air and back to the branch.

More trouble! A large male squirrel considered this branch his territory.

Chessie fluffed out her tail for a flight to the ground and ran away as fast as she could.

Screech! A car slammed on its brakes as Chessie dashed in front of it.

Safe at last on a high branch, she waited until nightfall,

then crept back to her nest, where she slept soundly, wrapped in her mother's tail.

The baby squirrels were now four months old and had grown quite big. Soon it would be time for them to live on their own.

As the warm June winds played with the leaves, the little squirrels left home. One by one, they disappeared into the greenery. Then one morning, as on every morning, Chessie headed down the beech tree and into the yard.

As on every morning, she dined on acorns and cleaned her tail,

and played tag and somersaulted with her pals.

Then, as on every evening, she came back home. But tonight her mother would not let her into the nest.

Chessie did not know what to do. Then she heard her pals chirping in the linden tree.

With a long, backward glance at her mother's nest, Chessie made her way slowly to the linden tree to join her pals. From the beech tree, the mother squirrel watched quietly as her last baby left home.

On her own now, Chessie went around the yard gnawing at the bark of the trees. She was leaving signs to let other animals know that this was her territory.

Baker, the family dog, could sniff around all day without getting tired. He smelled something interesting.

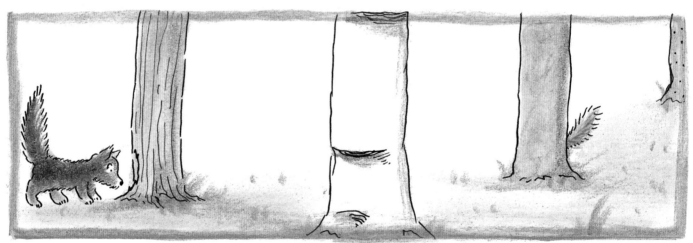

Sniff…sniff…sniff…

Baker was on Chessie's trail.

Aha! Baker caught up with Chessie, who was hiding behind a tree.

In the tree above them,
a fierce chattering arose.

It was Chessie's pals to the rescue! As Baker turned to see who was making the noise,
Chessie scampered up the tree to safety.

The three squirrels chattered and chittered in excitement. But wait a minute!
What was the wet stuff on Chessie's head?

It was rain, of course! And it was coming faster now as the wind began to blow.

Swiftly, the sky grew dark, and the strong wind shook the tree.
The rain poured down like a waterfall.

CRACK! BOOM! CRASH!

The thunder terrified Chessie and her pals. They clung to the wildly swaying branch, trembling with fear.

As suddenly as it began, the rain stopped, and the summer sun burst through the clouds.

Drops of water sparkled on the trees and flowers. Birds splashed in the puddles.

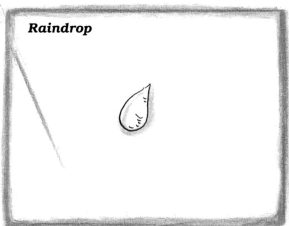

Raindrop

Seeds, nuts, and insects lay fallen on the ground. Chessie and the others had a feast. They dashed up to the treetops and then down again to dance in the shower of raindrops shaken loose by their frolics.

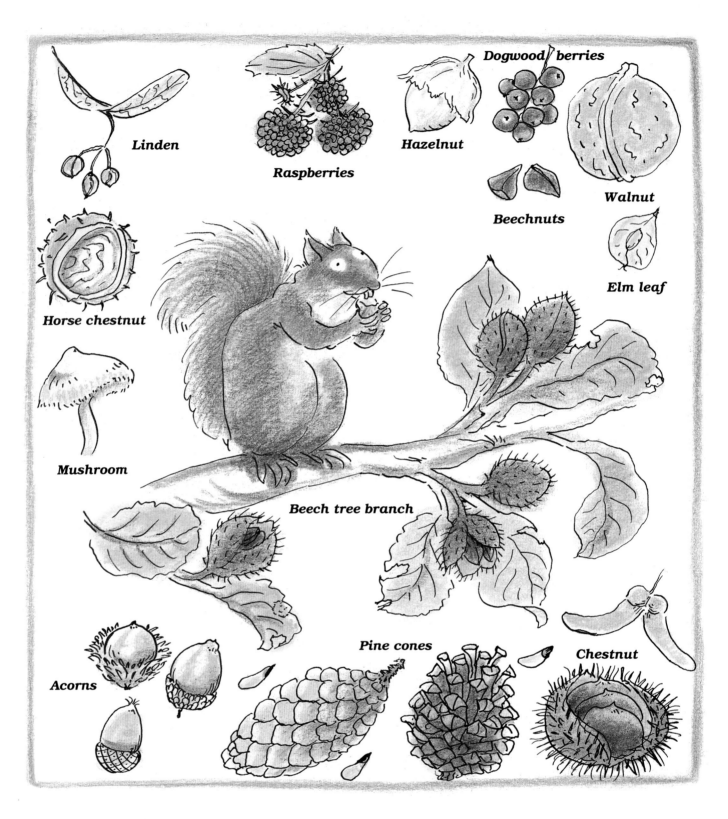

Linden

Raspberries

Hazelnut

Dogwood berries

Walnut

Beechnuts

Elm leaf

Horse chestnut

Mushroom

Beech tree branch

Acorns

Pine cones

Chestnut

Pine cone and pine nut

The hot summer passed and autumn came. Chessie sprang from tree to tree eating ripe nuts. Winter was coming, when she wouldn't find much food.

Chessie cracked the nutshells with her sharp teeth and ate as many as she could. Then she gathered more

and buried them in the ground.

With her keen nose, she would sniff the nuts out when winter came and dig them up. The honking of geese flying south for the winter made Chessie look up. She'd be staying.

Indian corn

In October, the green leaves began to turn colors — flaming orange, yellow, red, and brown. Then they began to fall.

The squirrels rustled through the dry leaves
looking for fallen nuts as winter grew near.

Kindling

November blew in on a cold north wind. It was time for the squirrels to find a snug winter home.

Chessie returned to her old home in the beech tree. But the hole was already home to several other squirrels.

An old nest in the pine tree would let in too much wind.
And squirrels can't camp with rabbits!

Or with raccoons! But Harry's place looked all right to Chessie.

She discovered a little hole under the eaves — and in she went.

Downstairs, a bright fire snapped and crackled, taking the chill off the gaily decorated rooms. On Christmas night, a freezing wind blew across the night sky. Snow had been falling for two days, slowly drifting higher and higher.

Outside, it was pitch dark, cold, and
quiet, but Chessie stayed snug in her
new attic nest.

 January arrived, even colder than December. Food was scarce.
Chessie raided the bird feeder, chasing away the birds to get at
the sunflower seeds.

She dug under the snow for the nuts she had buried and chewed bark off the trees.

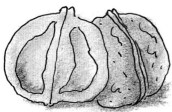

One day, Harry called to her: "Here, Chessie!"

He held out a walnut. Chessie snatched it with her paw. What a delicious treat! Every day after that, Harry brought Chessie a walnut when he came home from school.

February's days were bright and cold. When the sun shone, Chessie would sit on a branch and groom her fluffy, silver tail. She had grown into a beautiful adult squirrel.

Chessie chattered happily on her branch as she swung her tail slowly back and forth, back and forth. Soon, three male squirrels saw the pretty Chessie.

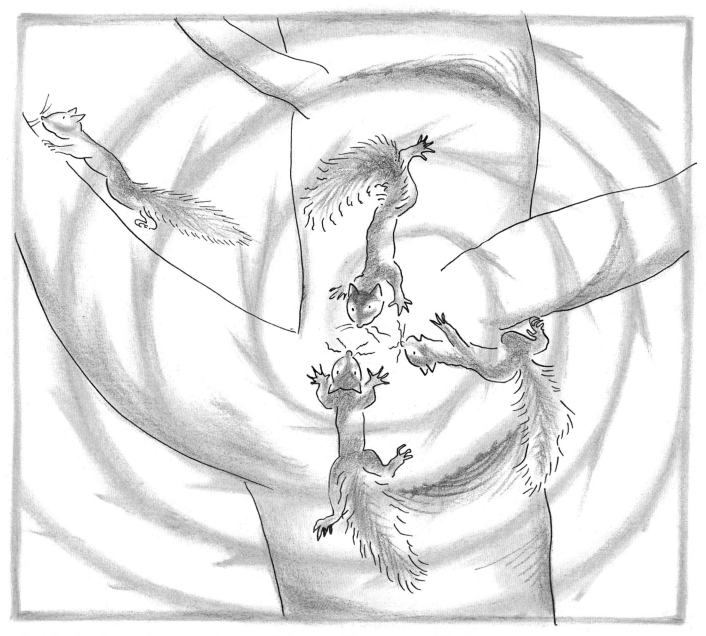

Suddenly, the male squirrels were fighting. The air was filled with the sound of claws scrabbling and scratching, and shrill screeching.

When the battle had subsided, one squirrel was the victor. He joined Chessie on her branch.

In March, the first signs of spring began to appear. The hard buds on the beech tree softened. The pussy willow buds swelled as the air grew gentler.

Chessie and her new mate sunned themselves on a branch of the beech tree.

The first robins had returned to the yard. They were
building a nest to hold the blue eggs that would hatch
into baby birds.

Spring was in the air, in the trees — everywhere. All
was just as it had been one year ago, when Chessie
was born.

Lily of the valley

In early April, five baby squirrels were born in Chessie's winter nest in the attic. Chessie had become a mother.

Chessie cared for her babies the way her mother had cared for her, nursing them, and licking them clean.

At night, the whole family slept wrapped in the father squirrel's big, fluffy tail.

Apple blossom

When May came, Chessie's family moved from the attic to a tree in the garden. There, Chessie taught her babies everything she had learned from her mother, starting with how to groom their fluffy tails.

Soon it would be time for Chessie to move
her family to a summer nest, just as her
mother had done one year ago. And then
Chessie's little squirrels would move out of
her nest into the green yard to begin their
first year.

Dogwood blossom

Raccoon's nest

Chessie's second nest in the maple tree

Oak tree where squirrels threw acorns at Baker

Chessie's third nest in the elm tree

The tire swing

Robins

The oak tree where Chessie was born

Baker

The black bird

The chestnut tree where Chessie met the big male squirrel

Rabbit's nest

The tree where Chessie met her mate

Chessie's fourth nest in the beech tree

Harry

Attic

Harry's room

Chessie's fifth nest in the linden tree

Where Chessie was almost hit by a car

Map of Chessie's neighborhood

Late afternoon is a quiet time to lie in the grass and listen to the scampering of tiny feet and the munching of tiny teeth. Then — chit-chit-chit! Hear Chessie's chattering as she teaches her babies how to clean their tails.